MW01127219

THE ULTIMATE GUIDE
FOR BANK DIRECTORS

Catherine A. Ghiglieri
and
Jewell D. Hoover

authorHOUSE®

AuthorHouse™
1663 Liberty Drive
Bloomington, IN 47403
www.authorhouse.com
Phone: 1-800-839-8640

First published by AuthorHouse 4/1/2011

ISBN: 978-1-4520-8817-4 (e)
ISBN: 978-1-4520-8816-7 (sc)

Library of Congress Control Number: 2010918158

Printed in the United States of America

Any people depicted in stock imagery provided by Thinkstock are models, and such images are being used for illustrative purposes only. Certain stock imagery © *Thinkstock.*

This book is printed on acid-free paper.

THE ULTIMATE GUIDE FOR BANK DIRECTORS

Foreword

The authors, former bank regulators, are the founders of the Bank Director's College. In these pages they present the essential information all bank directors need.

The manual provides two types of information:

- Official terms and stipulations from official sources (such as FDIC and Federal Reserve)
- A wealth of insight, including 'best practice' guidance, gleaned by the authors during their many years as bank examiners.

The Ultimate Guide for Bank Directors provides bank directors with the knowledge and insight necessary for performing their fiduciary responsibilities responsibly (i.e. conscientiously and effectively).

Acknowledgements

We are indebted to Mark Holland for suggesting that we write this book and for his help and support throughout the endeavor; to Mike Holland for the book photograph; and to Jay and Jeffrey Lawrence for their love and support.

We would also like to thank Barbara K. Lawing for the final copyedit; Lisa Dirks for the layout of the book; and John Wilson for creating the cover and overseeing the production of the book.

Catherine Ghiglieri

and

Jewell Hoover

Table of Contents

Truth in Lending
Equal Credit Opportunity Act
Home Mortgage Disclosure Act
Truth in Savings
Community Reinvestment Act
Flood Insurance

Chapter I

Banking and the Regulatory Framework

The Dual Banking System

The United States has a dual banking system, which means that a group wishing to organize a bank can obtain either a federal or state charter. The decision depends largely on the organizing group's strategic vision, business plan and/or desire to operate across state lines. If the group chooses a national bank, it is chartered by the Office of the Comptroller of the Currency (OCC). If they choose a state bank, it is chartered by the state banking authority where the bank will be headquartered.

The dual banking system began upon enactment of the National Bank Act of 1863. During the Civil War, the Act was passed, providing for national banks, whose circulating notes had to be backed by U.S. government securities. An amended act required taxation on state bank notes but not national bank notes. This effectively created one currency for the nation. Despite taxation on their notes, state banks continued to flourish because they introduced demand deposits.[1]

Competition between national banks and state banks comprises what is known as the dual banking system. This dual banking system applies to banks and thrifts.

---

1   Source: Federal Reserve Bank

REVIEW OF REGULATORY FRAMEWORK	
State Banks	State Banking Commissioner, FDIC or Federal Reserve
National Banks	Office of the Comptroller of the Currency
State Savings Banks	State Savings Commissioner, FDIC
Federal Thrifts	Office of Thrift Supervision

Figure 1

As shown in Figure 1, organizing groups seeking to open a financial institution can choose to become chartered as a state or national bank or a state savings bank or federal thrift. All of these types of financial institutions are insured by the (Federal Deposit Insurance Corporation (FDIC).

STATE AND NATIONAL BANK REGULATORS

All national banks are regulated by the Office of the Comptroller of Currency (OCC). While all national banks are members of the Federal Reserve System (Federal Reserve) and are insured by the FDIC, the OCC is their primary federal regulator. The Federal Reserve regulates national bank holding companies and the FDIC has back-up authority when a national bank becomes a serious problem bank or is designated as a troubled institution. However, if a national bank is not in troubled condition, it will generally only see OCC examiners in the bank.

State banks' primary state regulator is the respective state banking authority where the bank is headquartered and is usually called the Banking Commissioner's office for that state. State banks have the option of becoming members of the Federal Reserve and their primary federal regulator is dependent on whether the banks choose to be members of the Federal Reserve or not. If they *are* members of the Federal Reserve, their primary federal regulator is the Federal Reserve. If they choose *not* to become members of the Federal Reserve, their primary federal regulator is the FDIC. Regardless of the decision to be a Federal Reserve member or not, the Federal Reserve regulates state bank holding companies.

STATE AND FEDERAL THRIFTS[2]

There is also a dual banking system for state and federal thrifts, both of which are insured by the FDIC. If thrift is a state savings bank, its primary state regulator is the state banking or thrift authority and its primary federal regulator is the FDIC.

A federal thrift's primary regulator is the Office of Thrift Supervision (OTS). The FDIC has back-up regulatory authority for problem or troubled federal thrifts. The OTS regulates thrift bank holding companies much like the Federal Reserve does for bank holding companies.

History of the FDIC [3]

The FDIC was created in 1933 in response to numerous bank failures and a total loss of confidence in the banking system. Some drastic action had to be taken to restore public confidence. For a four year period between 1929 and 1933, approximately 9,000 banks suspended operations and 4,000 actually failed. The financial system was at a breaking point. Deposit insurance was implemented and at that time, accounts were insured for $2,500. That system of deposit insurance has been in existence since 1933 and the limits have been raised over time. When a bank is closed by the state or federal regulators, the FDIC manages the receiverships of failed insured banks and thrift institutions or finds a buyer for the assets. Failed banks are managed on a least cost resolution by the FDIC.

History of the Federal Reserve [4]

In the 1900s, when bank customers took out loans, they received their loan proceeds in the form of a bank note. Bank notes operated like currency and could be exchanged for gold or silver on demand. During the banking crisis of the Great Depression, people feared these bank notes would be worthless. The fear caused bank runs. Banks responded by trying to build up their gold and silver reserves and stopped making loans. This

---

2   Congress has passed legislation to merge the OTS with the OCC, but as of this writing the merger has not been put into effect.
3   Source: FDIC
4   Source: Federal Reserve

emergency mandated a stabilization of the banking system and a new form of currency.

In 1913, President Woodrow Wilson signed a federal law creating the Federal Reserve Act, which began the origins of the central bank system we have today.

History of the Comptroller of the Currency[5]

"In 1861, Secretary of the Treasury Salmon P. Chase recommended the establishment of a system of federally chartered national banks, each of which would have the power to issue standardized national bank notes based on United States bonds held by the bank. In the National Currency Act of 1863, the administration of the new national banking system was vested in the newly created OCC and its chief administrator, the Comptroller of the Currency. The law was known as the National Bank Act. One of the reasons Congress created a banking system that issued national currency was to finance the Civil War."

History of the Office of Thrift Supervision [6]

The Office of Thrift Supervision dates back to 1831 when several local town leaders identified a specific need for resources to buy homes. Resources were pooled to help establish the first savings association known as Oxford Provident Building Association. As these pools grew, members were able to own their homes and provide mortgages to others. By the 1890s, there were more than 5,000 savings associations nationwide. Many of these savings associations failed during the Great Depression and the federal government intervened with laws to restore confidence and continue a system to promote and support home ownership.

This last intervention established the Federal Home Loan Bank System. This was a system of 12 regional Federal Home Loan Banks that provided mortgage funding for savings associations nationwide. Congress then created the Federal Home Loan Bank Board to grant federal charters for savings associations and establish a regulatory system. The Federal Savings

---

5   Source: Comptroller of the Currency
6   Source: Office of Thrift Supervision

and Loan Insurance Corporation (FSLIC) existed to insure deposits for these savings and loan institutions.

Due to changes in deposit deregulation, Congress passed a law in 1989 that moved deposit insurance for savings associations to the FDIC. More recently, Congress passed legislation to merge the OTS with the OCC.

Role of Bank Regulatory Agencies

The banking industry is heavily regulated and governed by a series of banking laws and regulations. The primary goal of bank regulatory agencies is to ensure that banks are operated in a safe and sound manner and that they comply with banking laws. Because banks facilitate domestic and international trade, it is critically important that they adhere to strict regulations in order to maintain stability and predictability.

The role of each bank regulatory agency is to examine banks on a regular basis to determine if the banks are operating in a safe and sound manner and in compliance with laws and regulations. The bank's age, size and complexity determine how often an examination occurs. Banks that are newly chartered are known as *de novo* institutions and will receive an examination generally on a twelve-month cycle until their operations have stabilized. This stabilization timeframe is generally three years, but may be extended at the discretion of the FDIC or the primary regulator. Any bank that is designated *troubled* and those with total assets exceeding $1 billion will also receive examinations on a twelve month cycle. Banks with total assets of less than $1 billion and not considered *troubled* will generally be examined every eighteen months.

Regulators conduct both safety and soundness examinations and compliance examinations. A safety and soundness examination evaluates the traditional CAMELS areas: Capital, Asset Quality, Management, Earnings, Liquidity and Sensitivity to Market Risk. Examinations make conclusions on the institution's overall condition and risk profile and detail any matters that require the attention of the board of directors. A formal written Report of Examination is provided to the board with a requirement that they sign an acknowledgement page evidencing that they have read and understand the Report of Examination's contents. Reports of Examination are confidential and cannot be divulged by the board of directors to anyone outside the bank. Typically, the examining team will meet with the full board to discuss the examination's results.

The compliance examination tests for adherence to compliance laws and processes. Compliance examinations are generally conducted concurrently with safety and soundness examinations, but may be conducted separately and on a frequency dependent on the condition of a particular area of the bank. For example, a higher and more favorable Community Reinvestment Act (CRA) rating will provide the bank with an extended timeframe between examinations.

Areas typically reviewed under a compliance examination:

- Consumer Compliance
- CRA
- Bank Information Systems
- Bank Secrecy and Anti-Money Laundering
- Fair Lending

The Federal Financial Institutions Examination Council (FFIEC) is an interagency body under which the OCC, FDIC, Federal Reserve, OTS, National Credit Union Administration and the State Liaison Committee promote uniformity in supervision for both state and federal financial institutions.[7]

Function of Banks

The formal definition of a bank: *"an organization (usually a corporation) that accepts deposits, makes loans, pays checks and performs related services for the public. The Bank Holding Company Act of 1956 defines a bank as any depository financial institution that accepts deposits or makes loans".*[8]

Banks are the conduit for facilitating both domestic and global transactions. They also provide the means for the Federal Reserve to implement monetary policies that control the supply of money to control inflation and deflation.

---

7   The State Liaison Committee consists of representatives from the Conference of State Bank Supervisors (CSBS), the American Council of State Savings Supervisors (ACSSS), and the National Association of State Credit Union Supervisors (NASCUS).

8   Barron's Dictionary of Banking Terms

Hugh McCulloch, the first comptroller of the currency, in his letter articulating the principles by which banks should operate, wrote the following in 1863. It is still true for all banks today:

Every banker under the national system should feel that the reputation of the system in a measure depends upon the manner in which his particular institution is conducted and that, as far as his influence and management extend, he is responsible for its success; that he is engaged in an experiment which, if successful, will reflect the highest honor upon all who are connected with it, and be of incalculable benefit to the country; but, if unsuccessful, will be a reproach to its advocates and a calamity to the people.

Chapter II

Role of Bank Director

Banking is a heavily regulated industry. The process for obtaining a bank charter is complex and arduous. Once the charter is granted, the board of directors has a responsibility to safeguard the assets of the bank, maintain depositor and shareholder confidence and achieve profitability while operating in a safe and sound manner.

The board's role is to oversee the implementation of approved strategies that will safeguard assets while simultaneously achieving a profit for shareholders. These two things must be achieved within the framework of a safe and sound operation. Strategic decisions must be made in a deliberate manner and have an appropriate risk/reward balance. For directors to be able to manage risk, they must be independent in thought, and critically challenge and evaluate management assumptions and the bank's strategic direction.

The board is charged with overseeing the affairs of the bank. Oversight is not the same as managing the bank on a day-to-day basis. Daily oversight of the bank's operations is the responsibility of management. Since outside/independent board members are not physically at the bank on a day-to-day basis, their oversight is accomplished through a series of interactions with bank management, board and committee meetings, and a comprehensive management information system.

Selecting Bank Directors[9]

Bank directors are chosen for a variety of reasons including their financial expertise, business acumen, ties to the community, ability to capitalize the institution and strategic vision. While all of these characteristics are desired in every director, individuals bring different strengths to the board room and complement each other.

Whether the bank is in the organization stage or is an existing institution, the process of selecting directors should be overseen by the board's Governance or Nominating Committee. The committee should strive to achieve a balanced board with diverse experiences and skills, with the goal of having a majority board who are independent directors.

The Governance or Nominating Committee will establish guidelines for director qualifications, nominating process, background investigations, approval process and new director orientation. There should also be a process to determine if potential directors share and understand the core values of the bank, have demonstrated leadership abilities, are collaborative and are involved in the community.

If the bank is a public company, a majority of directors must be independent. For a director to be deemed independent, the board must affirmatively determine that the director has no material relationship with the bank directly or as a partner, shareholder or officer. Public companies must disclose the independent directors by name and discuss the basis for the board's determination.

Directors are not considered independent if any of the following apply:

- A director who is an employee, or whose immediate family member is an executive officer of the company, is not independent until three years after the end of the employment relationship.
- A director who receives, or whose immediate family member receives, more than $100,000 per year in direct compensation from the listed company, other than director and committee fees and pension or other forms of deferred compensation for service (provided such compensation is not contingent in any way on continued service), is not independent until three years

---

9   NYSE Rules for public companies

after he or she ceases to receive more than $100,000 per year in such compensation.
If during the prior three years:

- The director was affiliated with or employed by, or a member of director's immediate family was affiliated with or employed in a professional capacity by the listed company's present or former internal or external auditor;
- The director was employed, or a member of the director's immediate family was employed, as an executive officer of another company where any of the listed company's present executives serve on that company's compensation committee; or
- The director was an executive officer or an employee, or a member of the director's immediate family was an executive officer, of a company that made payments to, or received payments from, the listed company for property or services in an amount which, in any single fiscal year, exceeded the greater of $1 million, or 2% of such other company's consolidated gross revenues.[10]

Responsibilities of Directors[11]

Pursuant to case law or statute, directors are responsible for any decisions made regarding the bank's operations. Statutes passed by Congress prescribe how banks and boards are expected to conduct themselves. Case law is more difficult to pinpoint. However, two basic duties are well-known: the duty of care and the duty of loyalty.

Duty of Care

The duty of care requires directors and officers to act as prudent and diligent business persons in conducting the affairs of the bank. This means that directors are responsible for selecting, monitoring and evaluating competent management; establishing business strategies and policies; monitoring and assessing the progress of business operations; establishing

---

10   NYSE Rules for public companies
11   Source: FDIC

and monitoring adherence to policies and procedures required by statutes, regulations and principles of safety and soundness; and for making business decisions on the basis of fully informed and meaningful deliberation.[12]

Under the duty of care, bank directors are required to exercise the same level of care in making decisions for the bank that an ordinary person would use in making their own personal or business decisions.

The definition of the duty of care generally means the directors are expected to actively participate in board meetings and decision making by asking questions, ensuring that ethics are a part of the operations and setting an appropriate tone at the top. "Tone at the top" is a term from *Sarbanes-Oxley Act of 2002,* which means that directors have implemented an overall governance philosophy which mandates compliance with laws and regulations and doing the right things from a business perspective.

COMMON BREACHES OF THE DUTY OF CARE[13]

- Failure to adopt formal policies and procedures
- Permitting violations of law
- Failure to hold board and committee meetings on a regular basis
- Failure to attend board and committee meetings
- Failure to properly supervise management
- Failure to act on the recommendations of regulatory authorities

Duty of Loyalty

The duty of loyalty requires directors to administer the affairs of the bank with candor, personal honesty and integrity. They are prohibited from advancing their own personal or business interest or those of others at the expense of the bank.[14] The duty of loyalty requires directors to not use insider information for stock trades, conduct all transactions with the bank

---

12   FDIC Statement Concerning the Responsibilities of Bank Directors and Officers
13   Source: FDIC
14   FDIC Statement Concerning the Responsibilities of Bank Directors and Officers

at arm's length, avoid preferential treatment and maintain confidentiality of all information provided them at board or committee meetings.

COMMON BREACHES OF THE DUTY OF LOYALTY [15]

- Disclosure of confidential information to others
- Use of confidential information for personal or business interest benefit
- Failure to disclose conflicts of interest
- Violations of the bank's code of ethics policy

Business Judgment Rule

The Business Judgment Rule emerged from case law in the 1980s when there were a large number of bank failures and the FDIC instituted civil lawsuits against former directors and officers of failed banks generally for breaches of the duty of care and duty of loyalty. The Business Judgment Rule provides that the FDIC will not second guess the soundness of bank directors' decisions where they have proceeded in:

- Good faith
- After reasonable efforts to inform themselves
- Where they rationally believed that the action taken was in the best interest of the bank

The test concerning reasonableness of a decision is based on what a reasonable bank director would do in similar circumstances.

Today, most FDIC lawsuits are brought against directors who have been involved in insider abuse or where regulatory warnings have been ignored. Directors can minimize or eliminate legal and financial liability by adhering to the business judgment rule.

Corporate Governance

The term 'corporate governance' refers to the manner in which a company is directed by its board of directors for decision-making, delegation of duties and operational controls. The governance process also encompasses

---

15   Source: FDIC

interactions outside the bank with external parties including regulators, accountants, shareholders and the media.

With the high-profile collapse of companies such as Enron, WorldCom and others, there has been greater scrutiny of corporate governance and the manner in which boards of directors make decisions affecting their companies. The *Sarbanes-Oxley Act of 2002* was passed with the goal of restoring the public's confidence in the governance of public companies and financial reporting. As a result, there are many corporate governance requirements for public companies that also serve as best practices for non-public companies.

Corporate governance is perhaps more important than it has ever been as the public's perception of banking is arguably more negative than in years past. Recent polls asking whether certain industries do a good job or a bad job of serving their customers revealed that almost 40% of those surveyed felt that banks do a poor job. The following are practical suggestions for improving corporate governance practices for non-public banks:

SELECT AN OUTSIDE CHAIRMAN OF THE BOARD

Since the enactment of *Sarbanes-Oxley Act of 2002,* many boards have added an independent Chairman position. With this position held by an individual who is independent of the CEO, the board is not dominated by insiders and the environment allows for more open discussion. This change also allows directors to set an independent agenda for meetings that might otherwise be dominated solely by the priorities of management.

DISTRIBUTE BOARD PACKETS IN ADVANCE

Banks have various means of providing information to their board members ranging from regular mail to advanced technological distribution (e.g., email or access to a secure server). Regardless of the method of distribution, the information should be provided well in advance of the meeting to allow sufficient time to review the data and prepare for adequate discussion. In order for the directors to fulfill their duty of care, they must be prepared for board meetings by reading the information beforehand.

REVIEW BOARD PACKETS FOR RELEVANCE

Many board packets contain the same types of information and formats as they did twenty-five years ago. In today's environment, the information may be irrelevant, duplicative and not helpful in making critical governance decisions and/or reacting to changes in the financial services industry. Board packets for many banks have become unwieldy and filled with distracting and unnecessary information.

Good corporate governance requires a thoughtful and objective assessment of board packets to ensure that the information provided is relevant to discussions and decisions. The size, condition and complexity of the bank should determine appropriate content for the board packets.

When board packets contain information of lesser or no importance, the directors are distracted from focusing on critical issues. Certain core information should be presented concisely to enable the directors to supervise the bank in a competent and informed manner.

HOLD EXECUTIVE SESSIONS AT EACH MEETING

Public companies are required to convene executive sessions of the board without management in attendance. This is a best practice that should be extended to non-public companies as well. An executive session at each board meeting can be beneficial for the non-management board members even if the session lasts only a few minutes. The executive session provides a forum for discussion of issues without management and allows independent members an opportunity to obtain the views of others without the influence of bank executives. Additionally, bank executives will not become unduly alarmed because an executive session is taking place if it is a regular occurrence.

CONDUCT ANNUAL SELF-ASSESSMENT OF BOARD AND COMMITTEE PERFORMANCE

An annual board and committee assessment will help determine if the corporate governance process is effective. It also helps provide a benchmark for assessing director capabilities and determining whether the individual and collective skill sets continue to meet the board's strategic objectives. Suggested areas for assessment include:

- Decision making process
- Effectiveness of internal and external communications
- Risk control environment
- Compliance with regulatory mandates

- Board independence
- Board expertise
- Adequacy of strategic planning

REVIEW AUDUT COMMITTEE COMPOSITION

Public companies are required to have only non-management board members on the Audit Committee. The Committee must also have a financial expert such as a CPA or someone who can read and understand complex financial statements. This is a best practice that should be extended to non-public companies. While specific rules apply as to how independence is established, the primary rule is that Audit Committee members should not be bank officers or related to bank officers.

REVIEW COMPOSITION AND SIZE OF THE BOARD

Many bank boards have been together for years without any changes in composition. Some boards contain many members of one family, perhaps all related to the bank's CEO. Some boards consist of only the regulatory minimum number of directors, which are generally five. A review of the composition and size of the board may be in order. The ideal size for a board is between nine and eleven members so as to easily establish a quorum and to reach consensus and agreement on critical decisions. Boards of this size are ideal for constituting the necessary board committees.

Public companies are required to have a majority of "independent" directors, which basically means they are not officers or employees of the bank, not related to bank employees and have not been employed by the bank for the past three years. This is a best practice that should be extended to non-public companies. The addition of board members to attain a majority of independent directors will enhance the decision-making process of the board.

A certain number of board committees are necessary for the proper supervision of the bank. Most banks have Executive, Loan, Audit, Asset/Liability, Trust, Governance/Nominating and Compensation Committees. Small boards experience difficulty filling the committees because directors find it burdensome to spread themselves so thin. Expansion of the board to nine or eleven members allows the directors time to contribute in a meaningful way to the bank's supervision.

The collective expertise of a board should be evaluated to determine whether additional expertise is needed. For example, do independent directors possess banking expertise? Although a requirement for newly-chartered bank boards, this consideration is not imposed on existing banks, but perhaps should be. The board will want to be sure a CPA or financial expert serves on the Audit Committee and may need to add other expertise to other committees.

CONDUCT BOARD MEETING TRAINING

Many existing and new banks have never provided training to their board members. Training helps all board members fulfill their duties and responsibilities by providing a framework from which to make sound decisions. Training is critical for new board members, especially those who are not familiar with general corporate governance principles or the banking industry's many complex regulations. New member board training should consist of an orientation session as well as a training session geared specifically to new bank directors. Refresher courses for seasoned directors can be tailored to focus on such topics as the bank's business model, emerging risks, and changes in the regulatory environment.

Board Governance

The board and its committees should meet on a regular basis. "Regular" is generally defined by regulators as monthly or quarterly, depending on the nature and agenda of the meeting. Most small bank boards hold monthly meetings and larger and/or public banking companies typically meet quarterly. Regulators focus on whether the number of meetings allows for an acceptable governance process, and whether all board members actively participate.

Minutes of both board and committee meetings should be maintained as these minutes form the basis for how decisions were made by the board. Minutes also document adherence to the duty of care, duty of loyalty and the business judgment rule. Any discussions or decisions concerning insider transactions or lending limit approvals should be thoroughly documented in the minutes.

SEC regulations require that if any director attends less than 75% of board meetings, the fact must be disclosed in annual shareholder filings.

Even companies not subject to SEC regulations will want to ensure that directors are actively participating in board and committee meetings on a regular basis. Attendance in person is the best option for meeting this requirement; telephonic attendance is permissible if schedules prevent in-person attendance.

Committee Structure [16]

PURPOSE OF COMMITTEES

Board committees are the primary means for directors to oversee the affairs of the bank. They are designed to function by segmenting decision-making into smaller components. Committees also handle detailed matters and make recommendations to the full board for approval. The committees are generally small in size, containing three to five board members. Some board members may serve on more than one committee. Committee meetings occur either monthly or quarterly and detailed minutes should be kept to document discussions and decisions.

Committees should be governed by a written charter. At a minimum, the written charter should address the following:

- Purpose of committees
- Composition of committee members
- Rules governing appointment and removal of committee members
- Selection of Chair
- Delegation process to subcommittees and bank staff
- Legal responsibilities
- Specific duties and responsibilities
- Frequency of meetings
- Communication process with board

The following are the most common committees of the board:

EXECUTIVE COMMITTEE

---

16   Source Material for Purpose of Committees: American Bankers Association, Bank of America's Public Charter for Audit Committee, FDIC, Federal Reserve Bank of New York, Sarbanes-Oxley Act of 2002.

Generally, all important work and decisions of other committees are funneled through this committee since it serves as an overall umbrella for all committees and their work. The composition of the Executive Committee usually consists of the chairs of all other committees. Directors with specialized expertise (in finance or governance, for example), are sometimes included. On occasion, if the full board is not available, auditors and regulators hold meetings with the Executive Committee, which then presents the information to the full board.

AUDIT COMMITTEE

Since the enactment of the *Sarbanes-Oxley Act of 2002*, the Audit Committee has taken on greater significance. All banks are legally required to have an Audit Committee. For public companies, it is required that the Audit Committee be comprised of all outside directors and that at least one member be a financial expert (as defined by NYSE rules). Even for non-public companies, it is recommended as a best practice that the majority of members be outside directors, independent of management, and that a director with financial expertise also be included.

This committee is charged with oversight of the internal and external audit functions, review and approval of regulatory filings, financial disclosures and press releases concerning financial matters. Internal and external auditors should report directly to the Audit Committee, as opposed to management, to preserve auditor independence. Management should attend Audit Committee meetings in order to answer questions, explain other audit matters and participate in important discussions. Additionally, every committee meeting should include an executive session where committee members meet without bank management. These sessions should routinely include meetings with internal and external auditors and legal counsel without management in attendance. The committee should have its own access to separate legal counsel, as well as other consultants and experts, as matters arise that may require independent investigations.

LOAN COMMITTEE

The Loan Committee is responsible for processes and controls that will ensure acceptable credit risk. This function includes the development and approval of acceptable written policies to govern credit underwriting, exceptions, staff expertise and independent third party reviews of credit risk. Ideally, members of the Loan Committee should have some formal or practical experience in lending, as this is one of the areas that carry significant risk for the bank's balance sheet. Members of the Loan Committee will include bank staff members associated with lending as well as directors. The size and complexity of the financial institution will dictate how often the committee meets and what size loans it reviews and approves.

ASSET AND LIABILITY MANAGEMENT COMMITTEE

The Asset and Liability Management Committee is commonly known as ALCO. This committee is responsible for balance sheet management which includes funding, liquidity and interest rate risk exposure. Some financial institutions refer to these areas as the treasury function. Decisions are made as to how the institution will earn money and manage appropriate risk. Members of the committee should be familiar with funding strategies under various stress scenarios and should understand simulation models, assumptions, and risk parameters. ALCO usually meets on a quarterly basis, although many banks have a management component of this committee which meets on a more frequent basis.

TRUST COMMITTEE

If a bank has trust powers, it is legally required to have a Trust Policy Committee and a Trust Audit Committee. These committees ascertain the types of fiduciary services to be offered by the bank and oversee the process for compliance with laws and regulations as well as procedures to avoid conflicts of interest. These committees generally meet quarterly.

GOVERNANCE AND NOMINATING COMMITTEE

For public companies, the Governance Committee is mandatory pursuant to the *Sarbanes-Oxley Act of 2002*. This committee recommends nominees for board elections and adheres to a director selection process that includes acceptable qualifications/characteristics, background investigations, interviews and new director orientation. The committee is also responsible for management succession programs. Additional duties include ensuring that annual proxy statements are correct regarding director information, ensuring that directors' conflicts of interest have been disclosed and/or addressed in a satisfactory manner and that directors remain in compliance with all qualification requirements.

COMPENSATION/PERSONNEL COMMITTEE

The Compensation/Personnel Committee is responsible for Human Resource policies to determine compensation and benefit packages for all employees. It also determines compensation levels for Directors. Many new bank regulations have been enacted that govern compensation. The Board will need to be familiar with these regulations and their reporting requirements for financial disclosures. Compensation includes salary, bonuses, stock awards, profit sharing, deferred compensation, incentive programs and other similar plans. The Committee also conducts the performance evaluation of the President/CEO. This committee should consist only of outside directors to ensure independence and should rely on independent outside sources to determine if compensation packages are within peer group ranges and comply with bank regulatory requirements. Compensation and incentives should be tied to achievement of specific performance objectives and board-identified strategic goals.

Policies

Written policies and procedures should be in place for all operational areas of the bank. They should be approved by the board at least annually and noted in the minutes. Policies will reflect the bank's tolerance for risk taking and govern the risk control process. Policies should be written so that they are comprehensive, while providing for exceptions on a case-by-case basis.

Major policies all banks should have:

- Loan
- Allowance for Loan and Lease Losses
- Audit
- Personnel
- Asset/Liability Management
- Operations
- Insider Transactions
- Capital
- Code of Ethics
- Disaster Recovery and Contingencies
- Corporate Governance

Important Laws and Regulations for Directors [17]

Because banking is heavily regulated and most directors are not professional bankers, directors cannot be expected to be familiar with all banking laws. They should, though, have a general knowledge of significant laws that affect the bank's operations and should insist on compliance with the laws. Compliance with banking laws and regulations, as well as an insistence that employees adhere to ethical conduct, is commonly referred to as "tone at the top."

Generally, each bank regulatory agency (federal or state) enforces the same laws and regulations, but each agency's regulations contains different cites. This is because the regulatory agencies promulgate regulations simultaneously, but under different authorities.

Here is a list of significant banking laws:

12 USC §1829 –*Criminal Offenses Involving Dishonesty or Breach of Trust or Money Laundering or Pretrial Diversion Programs for Such Offenses* - The purpose of this law is to prevent the employment by a financial institution of persons convicted of criminal offenses involving dishonesty or breach of trust or money laundering, or persons who have entered into a pretrial diversion or similar program in connection with a prosecution for such offense.

12 USC §1831i –*Agency Disapproval of Directors and Senior Executive Officers of Insured Depository Institutions or Depository Institution Holding Companies* – The purpose of this law is to ensure that troubled institutions seek approval from bank regulators prior to adding any individual to the board of directors or employing any individual as a senior executive officer. A "troubled institution" is one that has a composite rating, as determined in its most recent report of examination or inspection, of 4 or 5 under the Uniform Financial Institutions Rating System or under the Federal Reserve Bank Holding Company Rating System, or is subject to a cease-and-desist order or formal written agreement that requires action to improve the financial condition of the institution.

12 USC §1831p –*Compensation Standards* – The purpose of this law is to prohibit excessive compensation to executive officers, employees,

---

17   Source: FDIC, Federal Reserve and OCC

directors and principal shareholders, which is considered an unsafe and unsound practice.

12 CFR §32 –*Lending Limits-Loans to One Borrower* - This is the OCC's regulation regarding loans to one borrower. Lending limits are restricted to a percent of capital loaned to one person or a related group of persons and/or business entities. Each state has its own *loans to one borrower* statutes and regulations and the limits vary from 15% to 25% of capital. The purpose of this regulation is to protect the safety and soundness of banks by preventing a concentration of loans to one person or a related group of persons who are financially dependent and to promote diversification of loans and equitable access to banking services.

12 CFR §215 –*Regulation O* - This Federal Reserve regulation is applicable to all banks and thrifts and governs any extension of credit to an executive officer, director or principal shareholder of the bank, any holding company of which the member bank is a subsidiary and any other subsidiary of that holding company. The regulation is written to ensure (1) that transactions are made on substantially the same terms (including interest rates and collateral) as those prevailing at the time for comparable transactions by the bank with other persons who are not covered by this regulation and who are not employed by the bank and (2) that the transaction does not involve more than the normal risk of repayment or present other unfavorable features.

12 CFR §364 –*Safety and Soundness Standards* – Banks are required to adopt policies and procedures to ensure they are operating in a safe and sound manner. This is the FDIC's regulation. See 12 CFR §30 for the OCC's safety and soundness regulation and 12 CFR §208 for the Federal Reserve's regulation.

Chapter III

Risk Management

Take calculated risks. That is quite different from being rash.

-General George S. Patton

Risk management is a term that means identifying, measuring, controlling and monitoring risk. There are generally nine categories of risk and the level of risk is determined by its impact on earnings and capital. The nine categories are as follows:[18]

- Credit
- Interest Rate
- Liquidity
- Price
- Foreign Exchange
- Transaction
- Compliance
- Strategic
- Reputation

The board of directors should appoint one person in the bank to be responsible for identifying enterprise-wide risks and reporting the level of risk to the board. This individual is usually known as the Chief Risk Officer and takes on the objective of controlling risk and assigning a risk profile that is consistent with board-approved tolerance levels.

---

18   Source: Comptroller of the Currency

Risk management has evolved into a concept known as Enterprise Risk Management and is a natural extension of the *Sarbanes-Oxley Act of 2002.* This concept is similar to a risk/reward strategy where the Board establishes risk and tolerance levels within an internal control environment. Enterprise Risk Management identifies risk throughout the organization and how risk in one line of business may affect other operations of the bank. Once the enterprise wide risk is identified, the Board will have a comprehensive view of business line interrelationships.

Management Information Systems

Any information is valuable to the degree that you can use it.

— Unknown

Management Information Systems, known as MIS, is the board's primary vehicle for receiving information. This information is used to make business decisions, assess the adequacy of management, make conclusions on the bank's risk profile and determine compliance with banking laws and regulations. The information is central to understanding key performance measures and trends. A comprehensive MIS system forms the basis for board reports. Information should be generated from an automated source versus manually prepared reports. This will help ensure that reports are accurate and reliable. It will also facilitate receiving the data on a timely basis. Acquiring and reviewing such information relates back to the requirements of the business judgment rule.

Many banks outsource their MIS to a third party vendor. To determine if a service provider is competent and reliable, due diligence analyses should be conducted prior to entering into a contract with the vendor. Banks should obtain the SAS 70 audit for a potential vendor as well as any financial audits. A SAS (Statement on Accounting Standards) 70 Review indicates the service provider has undergone a thorough and standardized audit of its control processes, often including its information technology.

Recommended MIS Reports

At a minimum, the board should receive the following reports at each board meeting:

1. Financial performance
2. Lending reports and trends
3. Asset and liability management
4. Deposit data
5. Capital ratios

1. Financial Performance Reports

Financial performance reports allow the board to determine if the bank is meeting its strategic goals consistent with budget and forecast models. The board should review the following financial performance reports at each board meeting:

- Key financial ratios
- Actual vs. budget performance
- Trend analysis
- Consolidated balance sheet and income statement
- Call Reports: Quarterly

KEY FINANCIAL RATIOS:

Key financial ratios measure the profitability and health of the bank.

Return on Average Assets (ROAA)

This ratio measures the profitability of the bank and is calculated by dividing net income by average assets. Most healthy banks have a ROAA of at least 1.00%.

Return on Equity (ROE)

This ratio is calculated by dividing net income by equity capital and measures the return on the shareholder's investment. Healthy banks have a ratio of between 12% and 16%.

Net Interest Margin (NIM)

This ratio measures the percentage difference between interest income on loans and interest expense on deposits and is calculated by dividing interest income less interest expense by average earning assets. The average NIM will fluctuate depending on the current interest rate environment.

Measuring the bank's performance against peers will provide an indication of the overall health of the NIM.

Earning Assets (EA)

Regulators will review the level of the bank's earning assets to ensure that the majority of such assets are working to generate profits. Regulators want earning assets to be greater than 90% of total assets.

Ratio Efficiency

This ratio measures how much it costs a bank to earn $1.00 and is calculated by dividing overhead expense by net interest income plus non-interest income. Healthy banks have an efficiency ratio of under 60%.

ACTUAL VERSUS BUDGET PERFORMANCE

Comparing actual to budgeted information allows the board to determine if management is meeting goals and if any negative trends are developing.

TREND ANALYSES

Trend data in graph form is a helpful visual representation of the key financial ratios and is often used in dashboard reports for the board's quick reference.

CONSOLIDATED BALANCE SHEET AND INCOME STATEMENT

This provides the banks overall balance sheet and income statement and should be compared to a corresponding period for the last fiscal or interim period. Budget versus actual data should also be included.

CALL REPORTS: QUARTERLY

Consolidated Reports of Condition and Income are known as "Call Reports," and are the quarterly reports that all banks and thrifts must submit to the FDIC. Three board members must certify by signature that the information contained in the call reports is accurate. The term "Call Report" received its name because in the early 1900's, the federal banking regulators telephoned the banks to request that certain financial information be submitted. Call reports today are submitted electronically to the FDIC. This data is available on all banks online at www.ffiec.gov .

Call Report data is categorized by the FDIC into various peer groups. These peer groups are determined by geography, asset size and number of branches. De novo banks have their own Peer Group and the group number is the same as the year the bank was chartered. For example, new banks chartered in 2007 will be in Peer Group 2007. De novo bank peer group data that is four years old is helpful to newly-chartered bank boards, as it shows how quickly new banks achieved profitability, and provides insight on the composition of their balance sheets.

2. Lending Reports and Trends

Various reports that provide data concerning the loan portfolio should be reviewed by the board monthly. Generally, these reports include the following:

- Portfolio composition
- Problem loans
- Delinquencies and charge offs
- Allowance for loan and lease losses
- Exceptions to policy
- Growth trends and other trend analyses

PORTFOLIO COMPOSITION

Portfolio composition shows the dollar amount and percentage of loans in each category, such as mortgages, commercial loans, consumer loans, etc. These reports can be further broken down into sub-categories such as commercial real estate and residential real estate. This information helps the board to assess the bank's risk profile and determine if management is appropriately implementing and monitoring Board-approved strategies.

PROBLEM LOANS

The level of problem loans is particularly important to track because of the impact on earnings and capital. Problem loans should be tracked by classification category with the large loans identified individually.

DELINQUENCIES AND CHARGE OFFS

Delinquency reports summarize the dollar amount and percentage of loans that are past due or have matured and remain unpaid. The delinquency report gives the board a gauge of the health of the loan portfolio. High delinquencies usually migrate into non-performing loans and losses that affect the overall ability of the bank to earn money and maintain adequate capital.

ALLOWANCE FOR LOAN AND LEASE LOSSES

The board must review the allowance for loan and lease losses (ALLL) every quarter prior to filing the bank's call report. This review is done to ensure the adequacy of the ALLL and the call report information. When performing this analysis, specific loans that are impaired must be identified and a loss factor applied. "Impairment" means there is a probability that either a portion or all interest and principal will not be repaid. Homogenous portfolios such as consumer, credit cards, automobile, home equity and residential mortgages should also be reviewed from a historical loss perspective and appropriate loss factors applied. Other important considerations to the ALLL include credit concentrations, economic conditions, staff expertise, demographics and strategic direction.

A good rule of thumb is the ALLL should generally be between 1% and 1.25% of total loans. This percentage will fluctuate up or down depending on the condition of the loan portfolio. A large number of problem loans results in a higher ALLL.

Loan Classification System

A bank's loan classification or grading system will serve as the primary basis for the ALLL analysis. All bank regulators use a four-tier system of classifying problem loans:

- Other Assets Especially Mentioned or OAEM
- Substandard
- Doubtful
- Loss

Other Assets Especially Mentioned

These loans have potential weaknesses that deserve management's attention. If left uncorrected, repayment of the loan could be jeopardized.

Substandard

These loans are not protected by the borrowers' financial worth, paying capacity or collateral and have a well-defined weakness that jeopardizes repayment.

Doubtful

These loans have all of the weaknesses of a substandard loan. In addition, these weaknesses make repayment or liquidation of the loans highly questionable and improbable. Examiners generally assign a 50% loss factor to these loan balances.

Loss

These loans are considered uncollectible and of such little value that it is not prudent to keep them on the books.

Each bank can develop its own classification system, which may contain many levels of pass loans, but each system should be similar to the regulatory classifications for problem loans.

EXCEPTIONS TO POLICY

Board–approved loan policies are adopted to minimize risk and to provide guidance to employees. Exceptions to any policy should be tracked so that the board can fully comprehend the risk profile of the bank. While the board sets the risk profile by approving the loan policy, loan officers can make exceptions to that policy within reasonable limits. The board cannot know the true risk profile of the bank without knowing the level of policy exceptions. Exceptions to policy should therefore be tracked as percentages and dollar amounts of the loan portfolio. Categories tracked should include loan to value exceptions, collateral exceptions, financial statement exceptions and loan underwriting exceptions, including appraisal violations.

GROWTH TRENDS AND OTHER TREND ANALYSES

Trend analyses are particularly helpful for the board to quickly determine if the loan portfolio is deteriorating or improving. Some boards use dashboards summaries while others use graph trend lines. Regardless of how boards decide to track growth and other trends, it is important that they review the information at each meeting and ask questions to more fully understand the impact on the balance sheet.

3. Asset and Liability Management

The asset/liability management reports generally consist of the following reports:

- Investment security reports
- Liquidity levels and trends
- Interest rate risk exposures
- Borrowings levels
- Economic data
- Benchmark reports on risk tolerance

The Board should review these reports to understand investment securities activity, liquidity levels, exposure to interest rate movements, level of borrowings and various economic data. The objective is to determine if board-approved strategies are being correctly implemented and to ensure that unacceptable risk-taking is not occurring.

4. Deposit Data

Reports regarding the deposit base will generally include the following reports:

- Loan to deposit ratio
- Deposit composition mix
- Core deposit ratio
- Brokered deposit ratio

LOAN TO DEPOSIT RATIOS

Regulators become concerned when a loan to deposit ratio is 90% or higher. A bank is generally expected to support its funding needs through core deposits, not through borrowings or rate-sensitive deposits. Typically banks fund their balance sheets through either retail deposits or wholesale deposits. Smaller community banks are generally retail-funded. This means deposits come from the local community and are not out-of-area or brokered deposits. Large banks that operate in multiple states are wholesale-funded. They have access to sophisticated capital markets and other wholesale borrowing facilities to fund their balance sheets.

DEPOSIT COMPOSITION MIX

Composition mix means the distribution of deposits in demand deposits accounts, NOW accounts, money market accounts, savings accounts, and other time deposit accounts. Banks track the composition mix because time deposits are more expensive than demand deposits accounts and affect the net interest margin.

CORE DEPOSIT RATIOS

The core deposit ratio is the ratio of core deposits to total deposits. Core deposit ratios usually include demand deposits, savings accounts, money market accounts, NOW accounts, and certificates of deposit of less than $100,000. Core deposits are those local deposits that will generally remain in the bank regardless of competitive interest rates. A ratio of 75% core deposits is considered to be a satisfactory level.

BROKERED DEPOSITS RATIO

Brokered deposits are those deposits acquired through brokers and dealers and are typically in denominations below $250,000 so as not to exceed FDIC insurance guarantees. Brokered deposit ratios are calculated by dividing brokered deposits by total deposits. These deposits are considered "hot money" or rate sensitive In order for the bank to maintain the deposit, competitive rates must be offered. Regulators restrict brokered deposits for problem banks.

5. Capital Ratios

Regulators view capital in three primary ways:

TIER I LEVERAGE RATIO

Tier I Leverage Ratio is the more traditional capital ratio and is calculated by dividing core capital by average assets. Core capital includes common stock, certain preferred stock, surplus, undivided profits, and capital reserves. This is the ratio most often used to reflect capital adequacy.

Generally, the FDIC requires de novo banks to maintain 8% Tier 1 Leverage ratio for three years, which is higher than minimum regulatory standards. The rationale for the higher ratio is based on the fact that de novo banks have increased risk profiles, thereby requiring higher capital levels to address unforeseen circumstances.

TOTAL RISK BASED CAPITAL

Total Risk-Based Capital establishes the amount of capital required based on the risk profile of the bank. Total Risk-Based Capital is calculated by ranking all assets according to a prescribed risk formula. For example, cash is risk weighted at 0% for obvious reasons. Loans might be rated 50% or 100% risk. The percentage is the amount of capital that must be carried for that asset category. The risk percentages are converted to dollar amounts used to arrive at total risk-weighted capital. Risk-Based Capital is the sum of Tier 1 capital and Tier 2 capital (subordinated debt, some preferred stock and the ALLL up to 1.25% of risk-weighted assets) divided by risk-weighted assets.

TIER I RISK-BASED RATIO:

The Tier 1 Risk-Based Capital ratio is calculated by dividing Tier 1 capital by risk-weighted assets.

PROMPT CORRECTION ACTION RATIOS			
Category	Total Risk-Based	Tier 1 Risk-Based	Tier 1 Leverage
Well Capitalized	>10.0%	>6.0%	>5.0%
Adequately Capitalized	>8.0%	>4.0%	>4.0%
Under Capitalized	<8.0%	<4.0%	<4.0%
Significantly Under Capitalized	<6.0%	<3.0%	<3.0%

Figure 2

The capital ratio chart in Figure 2 is used by regulators to determine which category applies for Prompt Corrective Action (PCA). PCA establishes minimum capital ratios and requires bank regulators to take prompt action when capital ratios fall below certain levels. Prompt corrective actions can include mandatory capital restoration plans or declaration of a bank's insolvency. These capital minimums do not apply when a bank is subject to an enforcement action. In those cases, regulators will require capital levels significantly above the minimum PCA levels. It is not unusual for a regulator to require a bank subject to enforcement action to have Tier I leverage to 8 or 9 percent before the bank will again be considered well-capitalized. If a bank is subject to certain formal enforcement actions, its capital level is considered to be adequately capitalized even though the percentage levels correspond to well-capitalized status.

Chapter IV

CAMELS

Bank regulators apply component and composite ratings to each bank based on the conditions found during an examination. These ratings provide an assessment on the overall health of the bank. All bank regulators use the same interagency rating system to arrive at the composite rating. The rating system is known by the acronym CAMELS.

- **C**apital
- **A**sset Quality
- **M**anagement
- **E**arnings
- **L**iquidity
- **S**ensitivity to Market Risk

Each of these areas is assessed by regulators before a composite rating is determined.

Composite Ratings

Composite or overall ratings are assigned during examinations on a scale of 1 to 5, with 1 being the best and 5 being the worst rating. The rating is disclosed to the bank in the Report of Examination. Each of the component ratings is also rated on this same scale. The ratings reflect the level of supervisory concern and the bank's level of financial performance.

COMPOSITE RATING OF 1

Banks in this category are sound in every respect and any issues identified during the examination are of a minor nature that can be handled in a routine manner. Banks in this category are considered resistant to economic and financial disruptions. One-rated banks pose no supervisory concern and may be examined on a less frequent basis, usually every 18 months.

COMPOSITE RATING OF 2

Banks in this category are fundamentally sound. They may suffer modest weaknesses that are correctable in the normal course of business. The type and severity of deficiencies are not considered material by the regulators. Similar to one-rated institutions, these banks are considered resistant to economic and financial disruptions. Two-rated banks pose limited supervisory concern and may be examined on a less frequent basis; usually every 18 months.

COMPOSITE RATING OF 3

Although the FDIC does not consider a bank to be in troubled condition until the rating is a 4, three-rated banks have a combination of financial, operational and/or compliance weaknesses that are moderately severe to unsatisfactory. Violations of law may also be present. While the possibility of an institution's failure is considered remote, the condition of these banks may deteriorate if corrective actions are not taken. Banks in this category may be vulnerable to adverse business conditions. Banks in the three-rated category will be examined more frequently, usually every 12 months with a 6 month interim review. Three-rated banks are usually subject to formal enforcement actions.

COMPOSITE RATING OF 4

Banks in this category have serious financial weaknesses and/or unsafe and unsound conditions. Unless corrective action is taken, there is a high potential for failure. The regulators examine these banks often and take the most severe enforcement actions.

COMPOSITE RATING OF 5

Banks in this category are likely to fail in the near term. Their weaknesses require an immediate injection of capital or the sale of the institution.

In the absence of additional capital or sale, failure is likely. Regulators will take additional enforcement actions, perhaps placing a supervisor or conservator in the bank. The FDIC may take steps to withdraw deposit insurance. Five-rated banks are considered extreme situations that require a virtually constant regulatory presence.

How Regulators Arrive at CAMELS ratings

What do regulators consider when they formulate the CAMELS ratings? They consider all factors that impact individual components of the overall rating, but especially the effectiveness of management and asset quality measurements.

Below is a look at each component of the CAMELS rating and what regulators consider in arriving at the composite rating.[19]

Capital

Regulators review any area of the bank that may impact the level of capital, including the following:

- Level of capital and compliance with PCA requirements
- Level of current earnings stream
- Overall financial condition
- Management and board oversight
- Sources of external capital
- Trend and volume of problem assets
- Concentrations of credit or investments
- Non-traditional activities
- Growth plans

---

19   Source: FDIC and OCC

Asset Quality

This area combined with the management component is given the most weight when assigning the overall composite rating. Regulators consider any area that may impact the quality of the bank's assets in determining the rating, including the following:

- Appropriate risk management controls
- Underwriting standards and policies
- Level and trend of problem assets
- Adequacy of the ALLL and methodology assessments
- Concentrations of credit
- Level of policy exceptions

Management

Regulators consider the quality of board and management supervision in determining the management rating. Factors considered include the following:

- Overall conclusions from other CAMELS areas
- Level of board and management oversight
- Level of noncompliance with laws and regulations
- Compliance with bank policies and procedures
- Adequacy and appropriate use of MIS
- Responsiveness to recommendations from regulators, outside consultants and auditors
- Management succession plans
- Reasonableness of compensation policies

Earnings

In determining the earnings rating, regulators review various elements including the following:

- Trends, stability and level of earnings
- Consistent sources of earnings
- Level of dividend payout
- Adequacy of budgeting and forecasting systems
- Interest rate risk exposure

Liquidity

When determining the liquidity rating, regulators consider the following:

- Funding sources, both internal and external
- Level of volatile sources of funding
- Trends and stability of deposits
- Management's ability to measure and monitor liquidity
- Contingency funding plans using various shock scenarios

Sensitivity to Market Risk

Regulators will analyze the following in determining the sensitivity to market risk rating:

- Level of and complexity of interest rate risk
- Use of simulation models
- Management's ability to measure, monitor and control interest rate risk

De Novo Bank Ratings

DE NOVO RATINGS	
Category	Rating
Capital	2
Asset Quality	2
Management	2
Earnings	3
Liquidity	2
Sensitivity to Market Risk	2
Composite Rating	2

Figure 3

Directors of *de novo* banks are often disappointed when they receive their first Report of Examination and realize they have been given an overall 2 rating. The ratings shown in Figure 3 are generally assigned to new banks. De novo banks usually operate at a loss for the first two to three years and as a result, there is pressure on capital. Although the management team is often comprised of seasoned bankers, they are operating for the first time as a singular unit and their performance as a team is unknown. Asset quality is also an unknown factor, as it usually takes 18 months for loans to "season". Until then, portfolio performance and payment history cannot be determined.

CAMELS Rating Exercises

CAMELS RATING EXERCISE #1

Study the hypothetical situation in Figure 4. Try to determine the ratings regulators would assign.

In determining the missing ratings components, consider that asset quality and sensitivity to market risk are rated 3. This means the loan portfolio likely has a significant volume of problem loans and the interest rate sensitivity is higher than average.

The management component rating would probably be a 3 because of the problems in the loan portfolio and sensitivity to market risk which reflects poorly on management's ability to measure and control risk in these areas.

RATING EXERCISE #1	
Category	Rating
Capital	?
Asset Quality	3
Management	?
Earnings	2
Liquidity	2
Sensitivity to Market Risk	3
Composite	?

Figure 4

The capital rating most likely would be a 3 due to the potential loan losses that would impact earnings and ultimately capital. The overall composite would most likely be a 3 since three critical areas received a 3 rating.

CAMELS RATING EXERCISE #2

RATING EXERCISE #2	
Category	**Rating**
Capital	?
Asset Quality	4
Management	?
Earnings	3
Liquidity	4
Sensitivity to Market Risk	3
Composite	?

Figure 5

In this second example, asset quality and liquidity are rated 4. The management rating would most likely receive a 3 or 4 because of the severe problems in asset quality and liquidity. Capital would likely be rated 3 because of the poor asset quality and the negative impact on earnings and capital. However, if large loan losses are likely, then a rating of 4 would be appropriate for capital. The composite rating would most likely be a 3 or 4, depending on the capital rating.

The regulators would likely take an enforcement action in the form of a formal agreement or cease and desist order.

Confidentiality of CAMELS Ratings

A rule worth remembering:

DO NOT disclose the CAMELS or composite ratings.

These ratings are confidential and can only be disclosed outside the bank in limited situations to the bank's attorneys, auditors and consultants. Disclosure of CAMELS ratings to unauthorized persons may subject the person disclosing the rating to criminal penalties.

Chapter V

Internal Controls and Audits

The trick is to stop thinking of it as your money

Unnamed IRS Auditor

Internal Control

A system of internal control processes must be implemented by the board of directors to safeguard the assets of the bank. The board of directors works with management to put the system in place. The board serves in an oversight capacity.

Internal Controls are necessary to comply with the banking industry's laws and regulations. Control safeguards take many forms, including segregation of duties, written polices and procedures, compliance with generally accepted accounting procedures and an overall acceptable risk control environment.

Organization of the Control Environment:

The board must approve and implement written policies and procedures for every operational area. This mirrors the concept known as "tone at the top."

Under this control environment, various delegation authorities and limits are established for such things as making loans and purchasing securities. Certain authorities above an established dollar amount will require joint board committee approvals or full board approval. Adequate risk control processes mandate segregation of duties and effective structures for measuring accountability. The compliance controls also require limits on purchasing and lending authorities.[20]

When two or more employees are involved in a transaction, the possibility of fraud is diminished. Segregation of duties means that no one person can control any transaction from beginning to end. For example, a loan officer should not make a loan and disburse the loan proceeds, nor should data processing personnel initiate and post transactions.

Rotation of personnel is a good idea. The practice provides control as well as training opportunities.

Personnel policies including hiring requirements, training, and job performance evaluations are important for control. All banks should have a vacation policy that requires employees to be absent for two consecutive weeks. This is considered an important safeguard to prevent embezzlements or other wrongdoing because when an employee or officer is absent from the bank for an extended period, any wrongful acts will likely be exposed. If the bank allows employees and officers to take less than two consecutive weeks of vacation a year, then appropriate compensating controls should be implemented to ensure that embezzlement or other fraud is not being perpetrated by an employee or officer.

Accounting Procedures:

The bank's accounting system should provide accurate financial records and be capable of generating useful information for the board. For example, general ledger records should be updated daily and show the bank's financial condition. Subsidiary records, such as loan and deposit trial balances, should be balanced daily with the general ledger.

Books and records should be designed to provide an audit trail (i.e. enable tracing of items through the general ledger system). Sequentially-numbered

20   Source: Comptroller of the Currency

instruments should be used wherever possible to aid in reconciling and controlling used and unused items. All accounting procedures should be in writing and cover all routine transactions.

Safeguarding Assets

Money is a strong temptation. Internal control procedures are designed to reduce that temptation in a variety of ways. For example, limits should be placed on the amount of cash in the vault and in the teller drawers. Tellers should have sole access to their own teller funds.

Common cash funds should be prohibited because there is no way to determine responsibility in the event of a difference or shortage. Procedures should be in effect for reporting shortages and investigating them.

Dual control is paramount. This means the work of one person is verified, approved or assisted by another. Two people should be required for acting on and approving certain transactions including vault opening, holds on accounts and dormant accounts.

Another control safeguard is adhering to strict employee hiring procedures, where credit checks and criminal and previous employment background checks are required.

Emergency preparedness plans also assist in the protection of physical assets by providing backup files for all critical records. The backup files should be stored off premises.

Internal and External Audit Programs

The board should implement effective internal and external audit program. The audit program will test the effectiveness of internal controls and provide the board with conclusions on how effectively risk control systems are being managed. Auditors must report directly to the board's Audit Committee in order to preserve independence. The audit function is the board's independent means of assessing of internal controls and compliance with policy.

During examinations, regulators review the audit program to ensure that the board has not delegated to management its responsibility for establishing and maintaining audit programs. The examiners review the adequacy of the internal and external audit programs, and the independence and competence of audit staff.

Types of Audits

There are generally four types of audits: financial, operational, compliance and information systems.

Financial audits review the general ledger, balance sheet and income statement to ensure the accuracy of financial reporting. Operational audits review the operations of the bank, including reconciliations of each account. Compliance audits encompass a review of consumer compliance laws. Information systems audits cover all data processing, privacy laws and data security.

Regulatory Requirements

Certain laws and regulations relate specifically to internal control and audit, including the following:

12 CFR §364- Safety and Soundness Standards[21]

This FDIC regulation prescribes the operational, managerial, and compensation standards to which banks should adhere. The regulation also addresses standards for asset quality, earnings and stock valuation that regulators consider appropriate. Implicit are the standards and requirements for internal controls and internal audit systems.

12 CFR §363 – Annual Independent Audits

This regulation requires banks with assets of more than $500 million or public companies to have an annual independent audit.

---

21   OCC's companion regulation is 12 CFR §30. The Federal Reserve's companion regulation is 12 CFR §208.

Chapter VI

Red Flags

When reviewing the MIS report in preparation for a board meeting, board members need to be able to identify red flags (indication that something could be wrong), especially in board reports.

This chapter will help board members determine which questions to ask and when to ask them. A red flag does not mean that something is wrong. It means board members should make inquiry about the issue and be satisfied with the response from management.

The board should request that management provide the bank's Uniform Bank Performance Report (UBPR) each quarter when it is published online by the FDIC. This report is formulated from Call Reports of all banks and contains peer group information that allows a comparison of an individual bank to its peer group.

Peer group comparison is one of the best ways to measure a bank's performance.

General Red Flags[22]

When board members identify the following in MIS (Management Information Systems) or board reports, they should ask management to explain the reasons:

- Bank ratios below regulatory minimums

---

22   Source: FDIC and OCC

- Bank ratios above regulatory maximums
- Ratios below/above peers
- Asset growth rates exceeding capital growth rates
- Ratios outside internal policy limits
- Excessive concentrations
- Sudden asset growth rates
- Large dividend payout ratios
- Increases in non-traditional activities
- Dependence on non-core funding sources
- Increase in litigation or consumer complaints
- Increase in employee turnover
- Unmet strategic goals

Red Flag Exercise

The following is an exercise to aid the directors in knowing when to ask questions of management. Below is a hypothetical case of a 25-year old bank with two branches located in a town with a population of 100,000.

Analyze the following red flag table. *Note the red flags in the shaded areas,* and identify questions that should be asked of management.

RED FLAG EXERCISE			
Category	Year 1 Your Bank (Peer)	Year 2 Your Bank (Peer)	Year 3 Your Bank (Peer)
Asset growth rate	8.00% (7.58%)	55.00% (6.90%)	46.00% (7.14%)
Loans	250,000	387,500	565,750
ROAA	.65% (1.15%)	1.87% (1.13%)	-.19% (1.20%)
ROE	7.80% (13.95%)	14.00% (13.89%)	-2.00% (14.00%)
NIM	3.30% (4.75%)	6.80% (4.68%)	2.90% (4.75%)
# of Loan Personnel	5	5	5
Loan personnel expense	350	600	650
Efficiency Ratio	59% (58%)	70% (57%)	80% (59%)
Loan Yields	5.86% (6.30%)	8.99% (6.25%)	4.99% (6.25%)
CRE Concentrations	10% (12%)	55% (9%)	75% (8%)
Brokered Deposits	15% (18%)	50% (17%)	45% (21%)
ALLL/Total Loans	1.10% (1.11%)	1.09% (1.15%)	2.50% (1.09%)
Past Due Loans	.50% (.56%)	1.75% (1.17%)	5.69% (.55%)
Non Accrual Loans	.60% (.59%)	.46% (.48%)	7.99% (.45%)
Loan Losses	15 (18)	250 (10)	1,738 (25)
Tier I Capital	8.99% (7.98%)	7.00% (9.00%)	5.99% (9.32%)
Dividend Payout	25% (22%)	68% (22%)	0% (22%)

ANSWERS TO RED FLAG EXERCISE

Asset Growth Rate	Board made a strategic decision to increase lending; 25 year old bank drastically increases asset growth rate of 55% in one year. Compared to peer banks, growth is a significant outlier. **Questions**: Is this the right strategy; what will be source of new loans; does the bank have adequate staff and expertise to implement strategy?
Loans	Loans increased $137,500 in one year; directors should ask questions concerning source of loans and quality of underwriting; Year 3 loans increased another $178,250. **Questions**: Is growth in line with strategic plan; what is quality of underwriting; how is staff adjusting to increased work demands?
ROAA	Historically the bank's earnings have been below peers; but with increase in loans, ROAA is 1.87%--much higher than peers. In Year 3, earnings are negative due to poor loan quality for Years 2 and 3. **Questions**: What factors contributed to historically low earnings; what weaknesses in credit administration have led to poor quality loans; how will the problem be addressed; what is the exit/corrective strategy?
ROE	Return on Equity has historically been below peer levels; trend was up in Year 2, but poor credit quality resulting in negative income forces a negative ROE for Year 3. **Questions:** Why was bank typically a poor earnings performer; is sudden growth the right strategy; what are the risks?
NIM	Net interest margin below Peer in Year 1 and significantly above peer in Year 2. The loans in Year 2 are of inferior quality and carry a high degree of risk. The high NIM of 6.80% in Year 2 is due to higher interest rates charged to sub-quality borrowers. Higher interest rates compensate for additional risk taken. **Questions:** Is quality being sacrificed for short term earnings; what level of risk is the bank taking; what is the profile of the borrowers?
# of Loan Personnel	Although the loan volume has drastically increased, the additional work is being done with the same number of employees. **Questions:** How can the bank maintain credit quality and administrative details with the same level of personnel; can the growth strategy be implemented with the same level of staff; what assessments have been made of staff expertise?

ANSWERS TO RED FLAG EXERCISE	
Loan personnel expense	Although the same number of lending personnel has remained constant, personnel expense has drastically increased. The reason for the increase is that loan officers were provided incentives for generating new loan volume. **Questions:** Did incentives apply to both quantitative (loan volume) and qualitative benchmarks (adherence to loan policy, monitoring loan portfolio risks, managing past due percentages, etc.)?
Efficiency Ratio	Increased overhead expense (incentive bonuses, legal fees for problem loans) has increased the efficiency ratio. **Questions:** What is causing the efficiency ratio to increase; have short-term gains in income taken precedence over long-term negative effects of asset quality?
Loan Yields	Although it appears that the loan portfolio is profitable due to higher yields, the bank is simply being compensated for the additional risk taken. When a bank has higher yields than peers, it is usually because of a higher level of risk. **Questions:** What is the bank's borrower risk profile and what exit strategy is achievable?
CRE Concentrations	Increases in lending are concentrated in commercial real estate. Not only are the loans of poor quality; but in Year 2 and 3, these higher risk loans represent 55% and 75% of capital. **Questions:** What is the bank's risk profile and effect on capital; what adjustments can be made; is there compliance with regulatory requirements?
Brokered Deposits	Hot money is funding the new loans versus core deposits. At some point, the bank may have to pay higher interest rates to keep the brokered deposits and the NIM and earnings will be adversely affected. **Questions:** Can short-term funding continue to fund long-term assets; what is the strategy for increasing core deposits; what is the effect of paying higher rates on the NIM; will there be regulatory restrictions on brokered deposits?
ALLL/Total Loans	By Year 3, significant loan losses require a higher Allowance for Loan and Lease Losses thereby affecting earnings. **Questions:** How many more problem loans are in pipeline; what is the quality of loan workout programs and personnel; what regulatory actions may be taken?

ANSWERS TO RED FLAG EXERCISE	
Past Due Loans	Problem loans begin to affect delinquency levels and they approach almost 6% in Year 3. **Questions**: What steps are being taken to reduce past due loans; where are the past due loans concentrated; is staff sufficient to work out past due loans?
Non-Accrual Loans	Non-accrual loans are almost 8% in Year 3. These are loans that are no longer earning interest and do not contribute to net income. Questions: Same as past due loans.
Loan Losses	Poor loan underwriting leads to loan losses in Year 2 and by Year 3, losses of $1,738M have occurred. **Questions**: Same as ALLL/Total Loans and Past Due Loans.
Tier I Capital	Tier I capital ratios are declining. Capital growth is not keeping pace with asset growth, and heavy loan losses and non-accrual loans have resulted in negative earnings for Year 3. **Questions:** What are the possible regulatory responses concerning prompt corrective action; what are the sources for external capital?
Dividend Payout	High dividend payout occurred in Year 2 because the ROAA significantly increased. By Year 3, losses and capital deterioration preclude dividend payment. **Questions**: What is the effect of stock value declines; how will the board contend with shareholder discontent?

Chapter VII

Surviving an Enforcement Action

When a bank is downgraded to problem status, the board faces the prospect of a regulatory enforcement action. After the initial shock wears off, management and the board have to face the realities of how to deal with and survive an enforcement action. This chapter provides a blueprint of what to do and what to expect.

What to Do When Being Informed that the Bank is a Problem Bank or in Troubled Condition

Problem banks have a 3, 4 or 5 composite CAMELS rating. Once informed of a downgrade in the composite rating, the bank should immediately review the Report of Examination and any materials the examiners provided and begin corrective action on each item. The more immediate progress the bank can make in correcting problems, the greater the likelihood that the enforcement action may be lessened.

What to Do When Being Informed of a Pending Enforcement Action

When the bank learns of a pending enforcement action, the first step is to call the bank's regulatory consultant or attorney and get that individual onboard as soon as possible. This person should be familiar with the enforcement process and with regulators in the bank's area. Determine that the consultant or attorney has a good relationship with the regulators and can negotiate the best possible outcome for the bank. This is not the time to threaten litigation, delay corrective action or strain relationships with regulators. Use the time wisely. Utilize optimum negotiation skills and implement action to improve communication and the bank's relationship with the regulators.

When regulators determine that an enforcement action is necessary, they will provide a draft of the proposed enforcement action to the bank for the board's review. At this point, the consultant or attorney should review with management each article in the proposed enforcement action. If actions have been taken to alleviate regulatory concerns, the proposed language in the enforcement action can be tailored to address improvements. The goal is to reduce the severity of the enforcement action before it becomes takes effect.

Types of Enforcement Actions

At some regulatory agencies, regulators decide on a particular enforcement action based upon the condition of the bank, the nature of the problems and the perceived willingness of management and the board to take corrective action. At other agencies, the regulators work within strict enforcement policies and do not have flexibility on the type of action required. They must implement the enforcement action dictated by the bank's composite CAMELS rating.

FORMAL ACTIONS	INFORMAL ACTIONS
Orders to Cease and Desist	Memorandums of Understanding
Consent Orders	Board Resolutions
Formal Agreements	Commitment Letters
Prompt Corrective Action Orders	
Capital Directives	
Capital Restoration Plans	
Continuing Condition Letters	
Civil Money Penalties	

Figure 8

Enforcement actions come in two types: formal and informal. As shown above, the formal enforcement actions are Orders to Cease and Desist, Consent Orders, Formal Agreements, Prompt Corrective Action Orders, Capital Directives and Capital Restoration Plans.

Regulators use formal and informal actions to address unsafe and unsound banking practices. An Order to Cease and Desist and Consent Order are the most severe enforcement actions the regulators can take.

Prompt Corrective Action is the framework that the regulators use to address banks that are not adequately capitalized. When a bank falls into the undercapitalized or significantly undercapitalized categories, regulators require that banks file a capital restoration plan. The regulators must take certain mandatory actions, including restricting payment of dividends, management fees, asset growth and brokered deposits. In some cases, limits are placed on deposit interest rates.

Capital directives are used solely to address inadequate capital.

When a bank is chartered, the FDIC establishes conditions for obtaining deposit insurance in a Continuing Condition for Order Granting Approval for Deposit Insurance. All conditions must be satisfied in order for the Continuing Condition to be lifted and deposit insurance approved. Some agencies' Continuing Condition Letters are known as Conditional Letters of Approval.

Civil money penalties assessed against the bank, directors, officers or institution-affiliated parties are based upon the seriousness and longevity of violations of law or unsafe and unsound banking practices. Regulators use a formal matrix to determine the dollar amount of the civil money penalty based on the seriousness of the issue and/or repeat violations of law or unsafe and unsound banking practices.

Informal enforcement actions are Memorandums of Understanding, Board Resolutions and Commitment Letters. Informal enforcement actions are used to address conditions that do not rise to a level warranting a formal enforcement action but still need to be addressed by the bank.

Regulators publish formal enforcement actions on their websites where anyone can read the entire document. Rarely do they make public the informal enforcement actions. Regulators also make public announcements when a board refuses to sign a formal enforcement action. The publication of these formal actions can subject the bank to both liquidity and reputation risk.

Because of the publicity surrounding formal enforcement actions, the bank should work quickly to reduce the severity of the anticipated enforcement action to the lowest possible level, i.e., Memorandum of Understanding or Board Resolution. To this end, the bank should enlist the assistance of its bank consultant or attorney from the moment it becomes aware that enforcement action is a possibility.

Tracking Compliance

The issuance of an enforcement action requires the board to create a committee to oversee compliance with each article. The task of complying can be daunting because of the number of requirements and timeframes imposed. Some banks will retain their bank consultant to monitor compliance with each item. Other banks use a spread sheet to track compliance. Regardless of the manner in which the bank tracks compliance, the objective is twofold: that compliance be monitored and ultimately achieved.

Care needs to be taken to respond to the regulators on each requirement by its due date. The timeliness issue ranks paramount in importance. Failure to comply with due dates will result in serious repercussions.

During the time the enforcement action is in place, regulators will be in frequent contact with the management team, including more frequent and longer onsite examinations. In addition, the bank will be subject to frequent and intense reporting requirements as mandated in the enforcement action and the reports of examination. For banks that are public companies, there will be additional SEC reporting requirements.

Management Studies

In order to correct the bank's problems, many enforcement actions contain a provision for a management study requiring an independent third party review of management capabilities. The quality of board supervision is assessed as well as corporate governance systems. Recommendations are made by the consultant based upon the conclusions of the study. The study is then submitted to the regulators for their review and approval.

Some enforcement actions require an enterprise-wide risk management study by an independent third party to identify the high risk areas of the bank, determine whether the bank has the necessary policies and procedures to handle these areas and determine whether there are sufficient management capabilities to correct any deficiencies and return the bank to a safe and sound condition. Board supervision and corporate governance systems are also reviewed as part of this broader management study.

The board of directors is expected to implement recommendations made in these management studies or discuss with the regulators why the recommendations will not be implemented. Recommendations range from management changes to management information systems enhancements. Organizational infrastructure changes may also be in order. Because of the seriousness of the outcome of these studies, the board must take care that the third parties performing the studies are highly qualified and independent.

Termination of the Enforcement Action

Some boards of directors and management teams become overly optimistic regarding the timeframes for achieving compliance with the enforcement action. Realistic goals help everyone work together more positively. The board should understand that regulators will probably not terminate the enforcement action for at least two years. Substantial compliance with the enforcement action is required and must be validated through at least one to two examination cycles to confirm that the bank's risk management systems are again functioning properly.

The bank will also need to achieve a 1 or 2 composite rating. Only then, with all milestones accomplished, will the enforcement document be terminated.

Chapter VIII

Compliance

A myriad of laws and regulations pertain to the business of banking. This Chapter focuses on the ones with which board members need to be familiar.

Bank Secrecy Act [23]

The Bank Secrecy Act (BSA) was passed in 1970 to mandate certain record keeping and reporting requirements to identify the movement of cash into and out of the United States. Bank regulators and law enforcement personnel use these records to identify money laundering.

There are certain warning signs of money laundering that banks should be aware of. These include increases in cash shipments, large numbers of cashier's checks or money orders sold for cash to non-customers for just under $10,000 and accounts with a large number of small deposits and a small number of large checks resulting in low balances. Bank examiners target banks for review if they have excess levels of cash or other indicators of money laundering.

To avoid money laundering schemes, the bank should have in place a comprehensive Bank Secrecy Act and Anti-Money Laundering Compliance Program.

---

23   Source: Federal Financial Institution's Examination Council

Bank Secrecy Act/Anti-Money Laundering Compliance

The Bank Secrecy Act/Anti-Money Laundering (AML) Compliance Program must be in writing and include a Customer Identification Program (CIP) to verify the customer's identity and collect certain identifying information about the customer when opening an account. The CIP should provide for verification of the new customer's name against terrorism lists. There are safe harbor provisions for sharing this information to protect the bank against the accusation of slander a customer is a suspect of terrorism. With higher risk customers, such as those in private banking, the bank should provide enhanced customer due diligence.

Suspicious Activity Reports (SARs)

Banks are required to file SARs with FinCEN (Financial Crimes Enforcement Network) in the following situations:

- Money laundering is suspected and transactions aggregate more than $5,000
- A bank insider is suspected (regardless of amount involved)
- Criminal activity is suspected and transactions exceed $5,000 and the suspect can be identified
- Criminal activity is suspected and transactions exceed $25,000 and the suspect cannot be identified

SARs are used to report bank robberies to local law enforcement.
There are also safe harbor provisions for filing SARS and the bank is prohibited from disclosing a SAR or even the fact that one has been filed in a given situation.

Currency Transaction Reports (CTRs)

CTRs must be filed for any currency transaction over $10,000.

With purchases of money orders and cashier's checks for amounts between $3,000 and $10,000, certain information on the purchaser must be maintained, but no CTR is required. If a bank determines that several smaller transactions are structured to avoid the $10,000 limit, a SAR must be filed. This practice of aggregating smaller deposits is known as "structuring".

For wire transfers of $3,000 or more, certain information on the requestor must be maintained in the bank, but a CTR does not have to be filed.

USA Patriot Act[24]

The USA Patriot Act is an acronym:

U niting and
S trengthening
A merica by

P roviding
A ppropriate
T ools
R equired to
I ntercept and
O bstruct
T errorism

In response to the events surrounding September 11, 2001, the USA Patriot Act was enacted. It criminalized the financing of terrorism and augmented the BSA framework by strengthening customer identification (Know Your Customer) procedures by requiring banks to practice certain due diligence procedures for opening accounts. The Patriot Act is meant to facilitate the exchange of information between financial institutions and the United States government on possible financing of terrorism or money laundering.

With the Patriot Act, banks gained added responsibility in four areas:

- Special due diligence when opening accounts for foreign banks operating in the United States

---

24   Source: Federal Financial Institutions Examination Council, OCC, FDIC

- Prohibition on correspondent relationships with offshore shell companies
- Mandated sharing of information with the government if a bank suspects that a terrorist or other banned foreign official or bank has opened a deposit account
- Requirements to "know your customer," which means certain types of documentary evidence are required to open an account (TIN, SSN, passport, alien identification card, etc.)

Truth in Lending

The Truth in Lending Act (TIL) or Regulation Z has been in effect since 1968. Its implementing regulation is 12 CFR §226. Regulation Z requires lenders to provide loan disclosures to consumers for such things as credit cards, car loans, and real estate loans. The purpose of the Act and implementing regulation is to provide consumers with the ability to compare the cost of credit from one lender to another and have all disclosures prominently identified.

Equal Credit Opportunity Act

The Equal Credit Opportunity Act (ECOA) and its implementing regulation, 12 CFR §202 or Regulation B, prohibit discrimination against loan applicants based on race, color, religion, national origin, sex, marital status or age. The loan applicant must, of course, be of legal age for entering into a contract.

The ECOA also prohibits discrimination against loan applicants whose income is derived in whole or in part from public assistance programs and applicants that exercise in good faith any right under the Consumer Credit Protection Act.

If the bank denies a loan, it must notify the applicant of the reasons for denial with what is known as an adverse action notice.

Home Mortgage Disclosure Act

The Home Mortgage Disclosure Act (HMDA) was passed by Congress in 1975. Its implementing regulation is 12 CFR §203 or Regulation C. This regulation requires lenders to report the race and gender of the applicant and the location of the property. If a loan is denied, the reason for the denial must be provided. HMDA assists regulators in assessing whether a lender is discriminating in its lending activities. This type of discrimination is often referred to as "red lining."

Truth in Savings

The Truth in Savings Act (TIS) and its implementing regulation 12 CFR § 230, or Regulation DD, requires depository institutions to make disclosures regarding interest rates paid on deposit accounts. It assists consumers in making meaningful comparisons between deposit institutions.

Community Reinvestment Act

The Community Reinvestment Act (CRA) was designed to encourage banks and other lenders to meet the credit needs of their communities, including low- to moderate-income neighborhoods. The Act, 12 USC §30, and implementing regulations require lenders to maintain a record of their efforts in meeting the needs of their delineated communities. CRA examination ratings are made public, unlike the CAMELS ratings.

Flood Insurance

Banks are prohibited from making loans secured by real property or mobile homes located in a flood plain unless covered by flood insurance. See 12 CFR §339.

CHAPTER IX

SIGNIFICANT BANKING LEGISLATION

Most often, banking laws are reactive. They are enacted to address an existing problem. Listed below are the primary laws that have shaped the U.S. banking industry.[25]

National Bank Act of 1864 – Established a national banking system and the chartering of national banks.

Federal Reserve Act of 1913 – Established the Federal Reserve System as the central banking system of the United States.

McFadden Act of 1927 – Amended the National Banking Laws and the Federal Reserve Act; prohibited interstate banking.

Banking Act of 1933 – Also known as the Glass-Stegall Act. Established the FDIC as a temporary agency. Separated commercial banking from investment banking, establishing them as separate lines of commerce.

Banking Act of 1935 – Established the FDIC as a permanent agency of the government.

Federal Deposit Insurance Act of 1950 – Revised and consolidated earlier FDIC legislation into one Act. Embodied the basic authority for the operation of the FDIC.

Bank Holding Company Act of 1956 – Required Federal Reserve Board approval for the establishment of a bank holding company. Prohibited

---

25   Source: Federal Deposit Insurance Corporation

bank holding companies headquartered in one state from acquiring a bank in another state.

International Banking Act of 1978 – Brought foreign banks within the federal regulatory framework. Required deposit insurance for branches of foreign banks engaged in retail deposit taking in the United States.

Financial Institutions Regulatory and Interest Rate Control Act of 1978 – Also known as FIRIRCA. Created the Federal Financial Institutions Examination Council (FFIEC). Established limits and reporting requirements for bank insider transactions. Created major statutory provisions regarding electronic fund transfers.

Depository Institutions Deregulatory and Monetary Control Act of 1980 – Also known as DIDMCA. Established NOW accounts. Began the phase-out of interest rate ceilings on deposits. Established the Depository Institutions Deregulation Committee. Granted new powers to thrift institutions. Raised the deposit insurance ceiling to $100,000.

Depository Institutions Act of 1982 – Also known as Garn-St. Germain. Expanded FDIC powers to assist troubled banks. Established the Net Worth Certificate program. Expanded the powers of thrift institutions.

Competitive Equality Banking Act of 1987 – Also known as CEBA. Established new standards for expedited funds availability. Recapitalized the Federal Savings & Loan Insurance Company (FSLIC). Expanded FDIC authority for open bank assistance transactions, including bridge banks.

Financial Institutions Reform, Recovery and Enforcement Act of 1989 – Also known as FIRREA. Its purpose was to restore the public's confidence in the savings and loan industry. FIRREA abolished the Federal Savings & Loan Insurance Corporation and gave the responsibility for insuring the deposits of thrift institutions to the FDIC.

Crime Control Act of 1990 – Title XXV of the Crime Control Act, known as the Comprehensive Thrift and Bank Fraud Prosecution and Taxpayer Recovery Act of 1990, greatly expanded the authority of federal regulators to combat financial fraud. The Act prohibited undercapitalized banks from making golden parachute and other indemnification payments to institution-affiliated parties. It also increased penalties and prison time for those convicted of bank crimes and increased the powers and authority of regulators to take enforcement actions against institutions operating in an unsafe and unsound manner.

Federal Deposit Insurance Corporation Improvement Act of 1991 – Also known as FDICIA. It greatly increased the powers and authority of the FDIC. Major provisions recapitalized the Bank Insurance Fund and allowed the FDIC to strengthen the fund by borrowing from the Treasury. It mandated a least-cost resolution method and prompt resolution approach to problem and failing banks.

Housing and Community Development Act of 1992 – Established regulatory structure for government-sponsored enterprises (GSEs), combatted money laundering and provided regulatory relief to financial institutions.

RTC Completion Act – Required the RTC (Resolution Trust Corporation) to adopt a series of management reforms and to implement provisions designed to improve the agency's record in providing business opportunities to minorities and women when issuing RTC contracts or selling assets.

Reigle Community Development and Regulatory Improvement Act of 1994 – Established a Community Development Financial Institutions Fund, a government owned corporation to provide financial and technical assistance to CDFIs. Contained provisions to curb "reverse redlining" where non-bank lenders target low and moderate income homeowners and provisions to reduce bank regulatory burden and paperwork requirements.

Reigle-Neal Interstate Banking and Branching Efficiency Act of 1994 – Permitted adequately capitalized and managed bank holding companies to acquire banks in any state one year after enactment.

Economic Growth and Regulatory Paperwork Reduction Act of 1996 – Modified financial institution regulations including those impeding the flow of credit from lending institutions to businesses and consumers. Amended the Truth in Lending Act and the Real Estate Settlement Procedures Act of 1974 to streamline the mortgage lending process.

Gramm-Leach-Bliley Act of 1999 – Repealed the last vestiges of the Glass Stegall Act of 1933. Modified portions of the Bank Holding Company

Act to allow affiliations between banks and insurance underwriters. Allowed national banks to underwrite municipal bonds and restricted the disclosure of nonpublic customer information by financial institutions. Made significant changes in the operation of the Federal Home Loan Bank System, easing membership requirements and loosening restrictions on the use of FHLB funds.

International Money Laundering Abatement and Financial Anti-Terrorism Act of 2001- Legislation designed to prevent terrorist and others from using the U.S. financial system anonymously to move funds obtained from or destined for illegal activity. Authorized and required additional recordkeeping and reporting by financial institutions and greater scrutiny of accounts held for foreign banks and of private banking conducted for foreign persons.

Sarbanes-Oxley Act of 2002 –Establishes the Public Company Oversight Board to regulate public accounting firms that audit publicly traded companies. Requires CEOs and CFOs to certify the annual and quarterly reports of publicly-traded companies. Required that insiders no longer trade their company's securities during pension fund blackout periods. Included whistle blower protections, new federal criminal laws, including a ban on alteration of documents.

Fair and Accurate Credit Transactions Act of 2003 – Also known as Fact Act. Extensive amendments to the Fair Credit Reporting Act to improve the accuracy and transparency of the national credit reporting system and preventing identity theft and assist identity-theft victims.

APPENDIX

This appendix has two parts: Resources and Abbreviations

Resources for Bank Directors

Comptroller of the Currency: www.occ.treas.gov

Conference of State Bank Supervisors: www.csbs.org

Federal Deposit Insurance Corporation: www.fdic.gov

Federal Reserve: www.federalreserve.gov

Office of Thrift Supervision: www.ots.treas.gov

Federal Financial Institution Examination Council: www.ffiec.gov

National Credit Union Administration: www.ncua.gov

Find your state's Banking Commissioner's Office at www.csbs.org

Abbreviations:

ACSSS	American Council of State Savings Supervisors
ALCO	Asset and Liability Management Committee
ALLL	Allowance for Loan and Lease Losses
BHCA	Bank Holding Company Act
BR	Board Resolution
BSA/AML	Bank Secrecy Act and Anti Money Laundering
CAMELS	Capital, Asset Quality, Management, Earnings, Liquidity, Sensitivity to Market Risk
C&D	Cease and Desist
CDFIs	Community Development Financial Institutions
CEO	Chief Executive Officer
CEBA	Competitive Equality Banking Act
CFO	Chief Financial Officer
CFR	Codified Federal Regulations
CIP	Customer Identification Program
CMP	Civil Money Penalty
CO	Consent Order
COO	Chief Operating Officer
CPA	Certified Public Accountant
CRA	Community Reinvestment Act
CRE	Commercial Real Estate
CSBS	Conference of State Bank Supervisors
CTRs	Currency Transaction Reports
DIDMCA	Depository Institutions Deregulatory and Monetary Control Act
EA	Earning Assets
ECOA	Equal Credit Opportunity Act
ERM	Enterprise Risk Management
FA	Formal Agreement
FDIC	Federal Deposit Insurance Corporation
FDICIA	Federal Deposit Insurance Corporation Improvement Act

FFIEC	Federal Financial Institutions Examination Council
FHLB	Federal Home Loan Bank
FinCEN	Financial Crime Enforcement Network
FIRREA	Financial Institutions Reform, Recovery & Enforcement Act
FIRIRCA	Financial Institutions Regulatory Interest Rate Control Act
FSLIC	Federal Savings & Loan Insurance Corporation
FRB	Federal Reserve Bank
GSEs	Government-Sponsored Entities
HMDA	Home Mortgage Disclosure Act
IAP	Institution Affiliated Party
IT	Information Technology
KYC	Know Your Customer
MIS	Management Information Systems
MMDA	Money Market Deposit Accounts
MOU	Memorandum of Understanding
NASCUS	National Association of State Credit Union Supervisors
NCUA	National Credit Union Administration
NI	Net Income
NII	Net Interest Income
NIM	Net Interest Margin
NOW	Negotiable Order of Withdrawal
NW	Net Worth
NYSE	New York Stock Exchange
OAEM	Other Assets Especially Mentioned
OCC	Office of the Comptroller of the Currency
OFAC	Office of Foreign Assets Control
OTS	Office of Thrift Supervision
PCA	Prompt Corrective Action
RBC	Risk Based Capital
RM	Risk Management
ROAA	Return on Average Assets

ROE	Return on Equity
RTC	Resolution Trust Corporation
SAR	Suspicious Activity Report
RWA	Risk Weighted Assets
SAS	Statement on Accounting Standards
SEC	Securities Exchange Commission
SLC	State Liaison Committee
SOX	Sarbanes-Oxley Act
SSN	Social Security Number
TA	Total Assets
TIL	Truth in Lending
TIN	Tax Identification Number
TIS	Truth in Savings
TL	Total Liability
UPBR	Uniform Bank Performance Report

INDEX

Duty of loyalty 11, 12, 13, 17

E

Earnings 5, 25, 27, 28, 29, 37, 39, 40, 41, 42, 43, 48, 52, 53, 54, 72
Enforcement actions 35, 38, 39, 43, 55, 56, 57, 58, 59, 69
Environment 14, 15, 17, 26, 27, 45, 46
Equal Credit Opportunity 64, 72
Examination 5, 6, 22, 37, 38, 41, 48, 55, 58, 59, 61, 63, 65, 68, 71, 73
Exceptions 19, 21, 29, 31, 40
Executive committee 18, 19
Executive officers 10, 11, 22, 23, 72
Executive sessions 15, 19
External 11, 14, 15, 19, 39, 41, 47, 48, 54

F

Federal Reserve 1, 2, 3, 4, 6, 18, 22, 23, 48, 67, 71, 73
Financial performance 27, 37
Financial system 3, 70
Flood Insurance 65
Function of banks 6

G

Governance 10, 12, 13, 14, 15, 16, 17, 19, 20, 21, 58, 59

H

History 3, 4, 42
HMDA 65, 73
Home Mortgage Disclosure 65, 73

I

Income statement 27, 28, 48
Information 6, 9, 12, 13, 14, 15, 19, 20, 26, 28, 29, 30, 32, 46, 48, 49, 59, 62,
     63, 64, 70, 73
Interest rate 20, 23, 25, 27, 32, 33, 40, 41, 42, 52, 53, 57, 65, 68, 73
Internal 11, 15, 19, 26, 41, 45, 47, 48, 50
Internal audit 48
Internal control 26, 45, 47, 48

L

Laws 4, 5, 6, 11, 12, 13, 20, 22, 26, 38, 40, 45, 48, 57, 61, 62, 67, 70
Lawsuits 13
Legal 13, 18, 19, 53, 64

CPSIA information can be obtained at www.ICGtesting.com
Printed in the USA
LVOW06s0704140814

398909LV00001B/2/P

9 781452 088167